MY WOODLAND PRAYER BOOK

is presented to:

_____

by:

_____

on this date:

_____

on the occasion of:

_____

Kendra Tierney

MY WOODLAND PRAYER BOOK
Traditional Catholic Prayers for Awesome Catholic Kids

Illustrations: Sarah O'leary

This book is dedicated to my children and godchildren. -Kendra

Kendra Tierney writes a Catholic blog at www.CatholicAllYear.com

Kendra's graphic design can be found at www.etsy.com/shop/PrintablePrayers

Sarah O'leary's artwork can be found at www.etsy.com/shop/Prettygrafikdesign

CONTENTS

Sign of the Cross 7
Apostle's Creed 8
Our Father 10
Hail Mary 11
Glory Be 12
Our Lady's Fatima Prayer 13
Hail Holy Queen 14
Rosary Prayer 16
St. Michael Prayer 17
How to Pray the Rosary 18
The Mysteries of the Rosary 20
Grace Before Meals 22
Grace After Meals 23
Morning Offering 24
Prayer to One's Guardian Angel 25
Angelus 26
Regina Caeli 28
Memorare 30
Prayer to the Holy Spirit 31
Prayer for the Souls in Purgatory . . . 32
Act of Faith 33
Act of Hope 34
Act of Love 35
Act of Spiritual Communion 36
Act of Contrition 37

SIGN OF THE CROSS

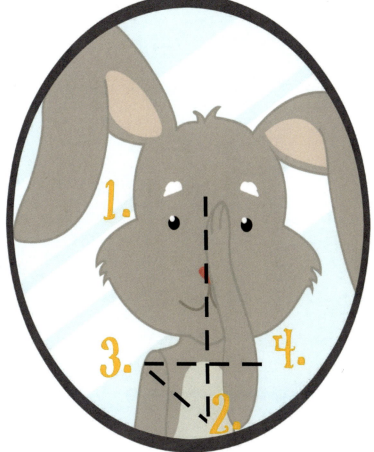

1. In the name of the Father, (touch forehead)
2. and of the Son, (touch chest)
3. and of the Holy (touch left shoulder)
4. Spirit. (touch right shoulder)
5. Amen.

THE APOSTLE'S CREED

I believe in God, the Father almighty, Creator of heaven and earth, and in Jesus Christ, his only Son, our Lord, who was conceived by the Holy Spirit, born of the Virgin Mary, suffered under Pontius Pilate, was crucified, died and was buried; he descended into hell; on the third day he rose again from the dead; he ascended into heaven, and is seated at the right hand of God the Father almighty; from there he will come to judge the living and the dead. I believe in the Holy Spirit, the holy catholic Church, the communion of saints, the forgiveness of sins, the resurrection of the body, and life everlasting. Amen.

OUR FATHER

Our Father who art in heaven, hallowed be thy name. Thy kingdom come. Thy will be done on earth, as it is in heaven. Give us this day our daily bread, and forgive us our trespasses, as we forgive those who trespass against us, and lead us not into temptation, but deliver us from evil.

Amen.

HAIL MARY

Hail, Mary, full of grace, the Lord is with thee: blessed art thou among women, and blessed is the fruit of thy womb, Jesus. Holy Mary, Mother of God, pray for us sinners, now, and at the hour of our death. Amen.

GLORY BE

Glory be to the Father,
and to the Son,
and to the Holy Spirit.
As it was in the beginning,
is now,
and ever shall be,
world without end.
Amen.

THE VIRGIN MARY'S FATIMA PRAYER

O my Jesus, forgive us our sins, save us from the fires of hell, lead all souls to Heaven, especially those who have most need of your mercy.

Amen.

HAIL, HOLY QUEEN

Hail, Holy Queen, Mother of Mercy, our life, our sweetness and our hope. To thee do we cry, poor banished children of Eve. To thee do we send up our sighs, mourning and weeping in this valley of tears. Turn then, most gracious advocate, thine eyes of mercy toward us, and after this our exile show unto us the blessed

fruit of thy womb, Jesus.
O clement, O loving, O sweet Virgin Mary.

V. Pray for us, O holy Mother of God.
R. That we may be made worthy of the promises of Christ.

Amen.

THE ROSARY PRAYER

Let us pray: O God, whose only-begotten Son, by his life, death and resurrection, has purchased for us the rewards of eternal life, grant, we beseech thee, that meditating on these mysteries of the most holy Rosary of the Blessed Virgin Mary, we may imitate what they contain and obtain what they promise, through the same Christ our Lord. **Amen.**

ST. MICHAEL PRAYER

St. Michael the Archangel, defend us in battle, be our protection against the wickedness and snares of the Devil. May God rebuke him, we humbly pray. And do thou, O Prince of the Heavenly Host, by the Power of God, thrust into hell Satan and all evil spirits who wander the earth seeking the ruin of souls. **Amen.**

PRAYING THE ROSARY

7.

6.

5.

8.

4.

3.

2.

1.

1. Holding crucifix: Sign of the Cross, Apostle's Creed
2. Holding first bead: Our Father
3. Next three beads: Three Hail Marys, Glory Be
4. Next single bead: Announce first mystery, Our Father
5. Set of ten beads: Meditate on first mystery while saying ten Hail Marys, Glory Be, Fatima Prayer
6. On each single bead: Announce next mystery, Our Father
7. On each set of ten beads: Meditate on next mystery while saying ten Hail Marys, Glory Be, Fatima Prayer
8. Center bead: Hail Holy Queen, Rosary Prayer, St. Michael Prayer, Sign of the Cross

THE MYSTERIES OF THE ROSARY

Joyful Mysteries

Said on Mondays and Saturdays

1. The Annunciation
2. The Visitation
3. The Nativity
4. The Presentation in the Temple
5. The Finding of the Child Jesus after Three Days in the Temple

Sorrowful Mysteries

Said on Tuesdays and Fridays

1. The Agony in the Garden
2. The Scourging at the Pillar
3. The Crowning with Thorns
4. The Carrying of the Cross
5. The Crucifixion and Death

Glorious Mysteries

Said on Wednesdays and Sundays
1. The Resurrection
2. The Ascension
3. The Descent of the Holy Spirit at Pentecost
4. The Assumption of Mary
5. The Crowning of the Blessed Virgin as Queen of Heaven and Earth

Luminous Mysteries

Said on Thursdays
1. The Baptism at the Jordan
2. The Miracle at Cana
3. The Proclamation of the Kingdom and the Call to Conversion
4. The Transfiguration
5. The Institution of the Eucharist

GRACE BEFORE MEALS

Bless us, O Lord, and these thy gifts, which we are about to receive from thy bounty, through Christ our Lord.

Amen.

GRACE AFTER MEALS

We give thee thanks, for all thy benefits, Almighty God, who live and reign for ever.

And may the souls of the faithful departed, through the mercy of God, rest in peace.

Amen.

MORNING OFFERING

O Jesus, through the Immaculate Heart of Mary, I offer you my prayers, works, joys and sufferings of this day for all the intentions of your Sacred Heart, in union with the Holy Sacrifice of the Mass throughout the world, for the salvation of souls, the reparation for sins, the reunion of all Christians, and in particular for the intentions of the Holy Father this month. **Amen.**

PRAYER TO ONE'S GUARDIAN ANGEL

Angel of God, my guardian dear, to whom God's love commits me here, ever this day be at my side, to light and guard, to rule and guide. Amen.

ANGELUS

V. The Angel of the Lord declared unto Mary.

R. And she conceived of the Holy Spirit. (recite Hail Mary)

V. Behold the handmaid of the Lord.

R. Be it done unto me according to thy word. (recite Hail Mary)

V. And the Word was made flesh.

R. And dwelt among us. (recite Hail Mary)

V. Pray for us, O holy Mother of God.

R. That we may be made worthy of the promises of Christ.

Let us pray: Pour forth, we beseech thee, O Lord, thy grace into our hearts; that we, to whom the Incarnation of Christ, thy Son, was made known by the message of an angel, may by his Passion and Cross be brought to the glory of his Resurrection. Through the same Christ, our Lord. **Amen.**

REGINA CAELI

Queen of heaven, rejoice, alleluia. The Son whom you merited to bear, alleluia, has risen as he said, alleluia. Pray for us to God, alleluia. Rejoice and be glad, O Virgin Mary, alleluia! For the Lord has truly risen, alleluia.

Let us pray: O God, who through the resurrection of your Son, our Lord Jesus Christ, did vouchsafe to give joy to the world; grant, we beseech you, that through his Mother, the Virgin Mary, we may obtain the joys of everlasting life. Through the same Christ our Lord. Amen.

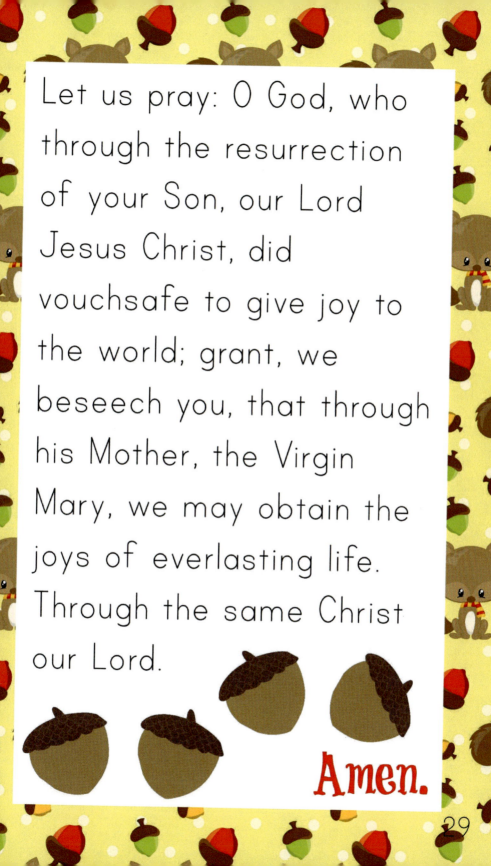

MEMORARE

Remember, O most gracious Virgin Mary, that never was it known that anyone who fled to thy protection, implored thy help, or sought thy intercession, was left unaided. Inspired by this confidence I fly unto thee, O Virgin of virgins, my Mother. To thee do I come, before thee I stand, sinful and sorrowful. O Mother of the Word Incarnate, despise not my petitions, but in thy mercy hear and answer me. **Amen.**

PRAYER TO THE HOLY SPIRIT

V. Come, Holy Spirit, fill the hearts of your faithful.

R. And kindle in them the fire of your love.

V. Send forth your Spirit and they shall be created.

R. And you shall renew the face of the earth. Let us pray: O God, by the light of the Holy Spirit you have taught the hearts of your faithful. In the same Spirit, help us to know what is truly right and always to rejoice in your consolation. We ask this through Christ, Our Lord. **Amen.**

PRAYER FOR THE SOULS IN PURGATORY

Eternal rest grant unto them, O Lord, and let perpetual light shine upon them. May the souls of all the faithful departed, through the mercy of God, rest in peace.

Amen.

ACT OF FAITH

O my God, I firmly believe that you are one God in three divine Persons, Father, Son, and Holy Spirit. I believe that your divine Son became man and died for our sins and that he will come to judge the living and the dead. I believe these and all the truths which the Holy Catholic Church teaches because you have revealed them who are eternal truth and wisdom, who can neither deceive nor be deceived. In this faith I intend to live and die. **Amen.**

ACT OF HOPE

O Lord God, I hope by your grace for the pardon of all my sins and after life here to gain eternal happiness because you have promised it who are infinitely powerful, faithful, kind, and merciful. In this hope I intend to live and die.

Amen.

ACT OF LOVE

O Lord God, I love you above all things and I love my neighbor for your sake because you are the highest, infinite and perfect good, worthy of all my love. In this love I intend to live and die.

Amen.

Act of Spiritual Communion

I wish, Lord, to receive you with the purity, humility and devotion with which your most Holy Mother received you, with the spirit and fervor of the saints. **Amen.**

ACT OF CONTRITION

O my God, I am heartily sorry for having offended Thee, and I detest all my sins because of thy just punishments, but most of all because they offend Thee, my God, who art all good and deserving of all my love. I firmly resolve with the help of Thy grace to sin no more and to avoid the near occasion of sin. **Amen.**

Editor and Layout Designer: Kendra Tierney

Copyright © 2018 Kendra Tierney
All rights reserved.
ISBN-13: 978-1987557138
ISBN-10: 1987557131

Illustrations © Prettygrafik.com

The prayers contained in this book are in the public domain.

Made in the USA
Lexington, KY
20 September 2018